DAUGHTER TRILOGY
by chiwan choi

*

BOOK ONE: ABDUCTIONS

BOOK TWO: THE YELLOW HOUSE

i lost my body / before i regained my name / before i learned to curl / my fingers tight enough / to keep myself from flying // i lost my body / but enlightenment never / came before i could / unfurl my terrors upon / the rough skin of this night

BOOK THREE

MY
NAME
IS
WOLF

i want to tell you / i want to begin

there was the apocalypse / you held it in your hands /
somewhere behind us / in a bar lads drunk / sang at the
top of their lungs / and their families / loved them // the
way you held it / until the silence came / like the darkness
before it / you smiled like a small past / and i wanted to
tell you / i wanted to begin / with my arms / wrapped
around you / eternally // so much has already been lost /
disappeared / this life of ours / of mine / already

today / i cried / for me / because / this thing / of mine /
named Body / is broken / and i can't / remember / when it
began / the first fracture / that gave / birth / to the life /
that followed // today / i cried / for me / in between /
strangers on / another / cross country flight / thinking of /
father / and mother / pointing outside / the small windows
/ of a pan am / flight / into darkness / telling me / to be
happy / of the uncertainty / to come / beyond boundaries
/ i was too young / to even know / existed.

out of time to confess that / this life as an immigrant has made me / my own family's other or that loneliness met me / in the front yard of our house in seoul / as i looked up squinting into the winter sun // the terror of moving here, to paraguay before that / was that i'd mistake threat for love / hatred for directions to that better life (a yellow house) // i've always been terrified of forests / because i lost my sense of direction long ago / as a child / in airports and hotel hallways / on stairways occupied by ghosts / and waiting rooms at the ER // i lost the map back to my body / when it (the body) began to crumble / how was i supposed to identify myself / in the fragments that were left behind? // but the forest — the winter too (and stairways occupied by ghosts) / is where i'm headed now / that's where you disappear / become the echo of a sound that / somebody, out discovering, thought they heard // three years ago i made my way to the therapist / and held my face sobbing / and i asked her what if the thing that i wanted most / was the thing i was most afraid of / what if what i longed for was the end / that lingers in the forest / like the sound of my mother / laughing at the kitchen window / as i stood crying in the alley / behind the house / convinced that i had lost myself / completely what happened to me / before i even learned to destroy / my life on my own? // i keep running into it / to see if i can catch / the moment it breaks / only to find the desire to speak / had already gone // my father's back is already curving / toward the mountain / they buried his parents / and mom holds my life / in her small hands / that rest on her lap // and brother is trying to hide / his illness // and in this place they are / looking at me / to me / like i'm supposed to know / as if i'm supposed to fucking know / what is coming / how to call it anything / but winter // i was 4 and it was korea / and i didn't know anything / other than home // it was morning and i ran outside / into the cold / because it was so bright / and in the yard / i looked up toward the sky / and squinted and my body / was shaking and my bones too / and she was there / the dog / hanging frozen from the balcony / slowly spinning // and i forgot the cold / i forgot what was happening / on my skin / in my body / because how was i to know / this is what they meant / by love and hope // today i am there again / i am a boy i think / or this thing of today that suffers

where once there was rage / it is now crestfallen // foggy nights / having trouble falling asleep / on the hood of a blue / toyota pickup / is more than mere time / away // reincarnation / takes so much air / meant for better beings / why do we get to return / to kill what survived us // the roads / are potholed with / our sins / littered with the stench / of all our previous versions // i wished for a child / to be the new shape into which / i could fit my life // and when she was gone / all that was left was / the sky / vast / empty

some days // there was food and love and some days /
the sun etching the loss of time on / your back. there
were tribes forming and fading // around me and the only
thing to know / was how to be ashamed of a life that
dwindles / until progress couldn't be measured. / the
world, we know, is on fire / this is my life of roaming /
until i can learn my name and become eternal.

it's february and february / is always trying to break / all of us / who are hiding under / the blankets / because it's too much / to remember all / the things we have lost // i want to stop writing / this book for a moment / to tell you that i'm ok / and that i'm also not ok // sometimes you set off / on a path that seems / so important / make yourself cry / by breaking the bones / in your extremity / tell your mother / that you are doing great things / that matter // the truth is somewhere / you shattered exactly / the way you were supposed to / no two pieces alike // i am so scattered today / the black birds in the air / stark against the white world / — in between seconds / you catch snow / falling up / this magic / is this a glimpse of what's to come // i forget your voice / more easily / than your scent / because your body / spoke louder / than your words // but forgetting / isn't always loss / sometimes it's / about finding your legs / again / about your hands / grasping at / your own life // let me come back / to this — // i am writing about dying / this narrator that walks into the forest / covered in snow and silence / like it is outside right now // and in this place of endings / the narrator meets a teacher / invisible / who teaches him / the names of the details / of his life // i have explained this before / but this part is for me / to remind me / because it is easy to lose myself / in my own journey // it's february / i tell my friend across the country / that februaries have been less / difficult since the medication / less not gone / just enough air / to make me believe / that i can find a way / to a kind of honesty

she calls / i am scared to answer / mom might tell me /
that someone has died // i avoid it / send her to voicemail
/ then pace around the apartment / fill a tall glass with
water / maybe even wash my face / with hot water //
intimacy / is an elusive beast / at the end of time — /
bodies breaking / broken / shattered / murdered // when i
call her back / she tells me she is praying for me / and
tells me to pray too / as i did when i was a boy / fighting
the demons in my head / my legs that kept crumbling //
my mother / she prays / and believes / still / that our child
will return / i don't tell her / that she already visits / from
outer space / entering my orbit / on plain nights / to
remind me to sleep / to put a sweater over my shoulders /
to tell me / that it's ok to lose the things / we needed to
love // she too (my mother) falls / moving from bed to
kitchen / the way I've fallen / and have kept falling / i am
of her / our fractures matching like trace / and i imagine in
her prayers / she asks for forgiveness / for what she
handed down to me // and in secret / i pray too / ask god /
why i wasn't given a chance / to be whole

my mother's hand in mine this afternoon / when i stopped
in for lunch of spinach soup / is the wall i drag the tips of
my fingers on / crying in the alley, my shorts wet / cuz i've
peed myself again / lost myself again / and somehow this
is not winter / like i remember every other day of my life
before 5 / before the moving and the abductions / before
the strange languages that will burn my tongue // she
believes the dreams gifted her by her god / as if i'm some
character she read about hundreds and hundreds of
times / in the old testament / those stories of times real or
not / when people were made to be salvation or
destruction / to that age of me when she believed in
something more / than broken bones and bruises that

appear at nights / speaking words she can't understand. // that she heard me crying in the alley behind the house / is a part of the story that i thought was important / but what does it matter that i was so close to home / when home was a word that would soon be taken from me and hidden in the snow to come.

will you point me to the field / long browned and fleeting / covered in snow that will not stop / relentless in its need to be // that field named Father? / i can no longer trust how i remember / his face or the texture of his palm / when he gripped my wrist to steady // how do the memories of him / and other bricks of my life / fade before he / they / is / are gone? // and the Forest asks, then how is it / that you will re-collect him // and i say, // because i will never forget the sound / his throat made when i caught him / calling for home what is it that you imagined / to hear at the end of knowing / at the cusp of happiness and belonging // god or something else invisible singing / a hymn to you for once / (with voices of strangers in unison in longing in something) // this morning you consider prayer / because you remember your father can't / properly tell you that he is dying / and how he stood in the elevator across from you / trying to measure the end of his life / by the number of blocks his legs can take him // and what came out were his arms toward you / like stumbling, his body moving toward you as if you / were gravity and the laws contained // you were told when you first learned / to want skin to call him father or the body / that hovers near your familar (whose name / they said was mother, was shield, / was home) // once again, you have been sidetracked / by faith while trying to accept death // come back // here is the lesson about names — // each one that your tongue / learned to love / were your fingers / wrapping / around shadows / that you knew / would disappear / with the light.

this is how i think it goes — / find someone who will replace all the things i fear about dying, / until their bones too shatter in regret / as i step out into the first sun after winter and breathe. // my father, you see, is crying somewhere in LA because / his little brother has died in korea and he can't fly there to mourn. / they were like twins. i mistook one for the other once before / they took me to the mountain and i then mistook grandmother's grave for a mountain. // what i'm trying to say is that i walked through new york today like / a familiar ghost and turned left around a new coffee shop where / a person with brown skin once stood loving. // and around the corner were the trees and the silence and the snow / that covered the whole of it and winter / spoke to me again asking me to name my body / to name my mother to name the hours clutched in my hands / like such rocks scooped up from the bottom of the river.

but i / fell in love with the life of us / that we dreamt up — / an apartment high up above the world / light through the walls of windows / heating our bodies / our children running through the city / catching their first trains // with love / came the forgetting / of the one we had where / nights break in shivers and the wailing / rising from a depth that can't be / traced to childhood / this one where we scream at / each other in a half empty bar / because we are so afraid of giving up // but i / saw a perfect light above st. louis / and it shattered bones, shell, chains / hard things that hold me up or in place / making that sound like whimpering // now standing under an awning / the rain falling without malice / i drift away again / to want: // in the living room / warm enough for t-shirts. / there is music / because there is always a dying / and we are standing somewhere / between the couch / and the dining table // my face / worn / recognizes your hand / as the place we began / while i place my own hands / on your waist / to dance / slow / with feet bare / on the wooden floor / as outside / winter continues to / do its work.

i held my arms out in front of me / the way we practiced in elementary school / before i could even learn this language ' my hands on the shoulders of the kid ahead of me / measuring the distance to keep from each other / arm length, the impossible distance of the air in reaching // the snow then fell remaking my skin / into a winter river a month from thaw / from exposing the heart that has never stopped breaking / time long ago untracked until we can't know / whether it's the fire or the drowning that will greet us // when i was a child father would point at every breath / in the room and tell me to learn to identify the ones / that are here to kill me, but now he is small / and full of bread and is only afraid / that i'll speak too much // this is the forest / that much i know / because my bones remember / how to be scared among the trees // they gave the history of our skin to jesus / so i would choose to erase my own name // this is where i have come / to pretend these trees are shadows of my mother / shuffling across the front yard, the dog close by / following, her gloved hands tending to the rose bushes / that she'd hoped one day would bloom something other / than grief // and that this forest will be the room with the white walls / in which i could break like daylight, like silence, like promise

you map my body / until i remember // that it was always /
this journey to death // you pave the roads / until i
remember // to look out the window / at the sky that may
be god // you trace my skin / until i remember // that i was
always / meant to call the final place home // you make
me remember / i was meant to dance // and hang on to
death / like my beloved // you make me remember my
body / then help me forget

they called it prison / but it was your skin. // they called it
progress / while breaking your bones. // you said blame /
but it was your heart. // i will call it today / these seconds
that i lose / on your shoulders. // i will call her mother /
who searches my face for her childhood // i will call it
father / this body dissolving // where were you tuesday /
when i called your name // i held on to her arm / before i
knew to call it bridge // that was love in the front yard /
that she called opium // you called my name / when i
reached for the dirt.

this morning in secret / when you put on my shirt / did my skin speak to you, tell you / this: what i know is / the dark universe that // always held this secret / between us from us / that for most of this life / i didn't know how to be / what god or chance meant for me // when you put your scent on / this surface which i could reach / i heard you say to me: breathe / and tell me how it / feels to learn that what / you love is saving you.

when did you learn / to hold a body in transit / from joy to a splintered curl / of a scream born in / the silent heart of a sundown? // were you only trying / to transfer the weight / of their bricks of bones / until you could feel / less translucent? // what you hear here / as your skin burns its last / fires is the sound of your life / circling back in ways / your parents didn't have a language to explain — / all those highlighted words / in the king james bible they gave you / on your 18th birthday and told / you to mark up in different color / for each time you read through the / whole of it // it wasn't god or teaching / or the path to forgiveness. // they were just desperate / to tell you / that you matter / in this world.

i didn't know / that learning to love / another // was braiding lives / together / intertwining / to keep / from unraveling // but the trauma / isn't without weight / and bones fray / with breathing // i am slow / to learn / and i don't know how / now / to fall // without collapsing / the world around me / having tied / so tight / all that i have hoped / around my bones.

as you spoke, your voice bouncing / from the bare branches all around me / i thought of my first days / on this land or the first ones / i have held on to. there was // a sun like i hadn't known that made / my skin so yellow naked. / everything felt so close to me / and it made me afraid / of being known. in the periphery / i remember now as your voice reaches / me were those things that i noticed / for the first time to be pulsing / like life and the moment before sleep / — your voice now that calls my name wolf / in teaching you / i too am saved. // we save each other / so we can die together. / that is how we win.

when the cold came / I walked into the forest to die /
because winter was always the season / I knew how to
love // there was once a tribe / that was turned into a river
/ of blood, the current soaking my feet / until i chose to
walk again hidden from the sun. // it seems like so many
years ago / that my father told me / one day i would learn
to accept / loneliness and that there was a place for me
where fruits ripen / on the branches that also hold up the
sky / in anger. // there comes a day / when your eyes can
no longer / stare at your brother at your sister / burying
teeth into their own skin / to find a chance to escape the
curse / of their bodies // maybe we don't realize we have /
walked away from our lives until / we are standing in
snow falling / like childhood and front yards and your /
first broken bone / learning that white was always the
color of death.

outside it was white. / the color had no purpose / it was
just the nature of it // it was snow and it was winter and
the freezing of time / this white of the season / learned to
kill in its meeting of my skin // how am i to ask something
/ falling without thought / to have mercy when the fault /
was my body existing / as more than a remnant / of war
like the gutted bones / of homes where lives huddled // if i
had just been born as one of these hard things / that
could withstand it all: the cold, the silence, / the
whiteness // because it had already given up / this foolish
will to wait for the warmth / to come and stay.

it's winter. my skin tells me. / and my heart? something
about goodbye. // what was it that you wanted? / for me
to ask to be saved? // i know you. // it is you, winter / and
you have come for me.

in the air / you can't breathe without / shelter, without prison / without another kind / of living. // i am a shadow / over broken terrain / on surface like skin / that taught itself / to heal too much. // on the 13th of this month / they will tell my father / to split open his chest / and pretend death isn't coming / and somewhere across / this country i will / catch a moment / where a yellow flower / braces itself from winter by opening. // is it here, i ask the forest, / where everything changes / where the light touches my heart / in the cold night shifting / and she said, open your mouth / to what you know of as god / there are so many voices / within you that want / to be saved.

there were bodies / close to each other / tight enough / to smell the whiskey / rising from skin / burning in joy. // we called each other's / names through our eyes / that weren't afraid / to flood. // it was just a night / in a city / that would both / pass through darkness / and into the sun // but there was / a moment / under a low ceiling / in el sereno / when we / all of us / were invincible.

you learned to be afraid / before you ever had a chance to believe / that death was not an enemy / but your birthright. you believed it when / the snow fell for the first time / and you feared the invisibility of you as you howled. // i will lead you to your name / death will still come / because you will have earned it / and it will be yours as it always was. // we will begin with / what's beneath your feet. / its name is soil. / this is land. / this is the ground. // this is the open palms / of the universe / as it holds you / up in worship.

at 5 i was taught that everything is temporary / his hands holding my face (in my memory) / leaving me chasing what have dissolved / until one day i am 16 / under the covers for the sixth straight day / the impossibility of leaving my room, my mother on the other side of the door / her hurt voice pleading with my brother, telling him that / i was crazy and that she couldn't wait til i was old enough to disappear / (the way my home and the soil that i grew out of / and the snow on the swing in the yard and the dog / frozen dangling from the balcony all disappear). / tonight there is a new snow (wait it too is gone) / and i'm thinking of that morning again and there is no mother or brother outside my room this time / it is just me under that blanket, my clothes soaked in days of sweat / curled up in a ball, telling myself over and over / ...*you are crazy you are crazy and i can't wait til you are gone til you disappear til you are something that can never be found.*

i went outside yesterday / and was disappointed / it looked like how i remembered it / but with more people in line / at the rite aid. otherwise the same: / people not wanting to die / but very willing to kill // it was easy to detach from it all / this morning when i woke up and read the news / something about white men and murders / it is easy to detach when the dead / scream like me, made of familiar skin // i will feel this too later while / standing in the kitchen with a glass of water / and consider my mother who brought us here / on father's stubborn whims // what am i to be today — / angry / sad / loud / somewhere between bleeding because i'm alive / and bleeding because you have taken my life // the noise is unbearable here and now / maybe it's still just in my head / going through my crazies, as mom used to say / whenever i scared her by sleeping / too much or too little // i am tired and i want to sleep / for a long long time // i am tired and i have been too afraid to sleep / for longer than that.

what does it feel like / in my head / this day of wanting
nothing more / than to stop to stop to find comfort / under
the blanket — sniffing for my own scent / to find where i
went wrong all went wrong / there's a story i've been
making / in my head / about an old man that looks like
me / whose power is to leave permanent footsteps / and
one impossible weekend / he drags his body
backtracking / each and every one of those marks / to
find the splinters his bone left behind / (it is not 5am
again and outside / there are sounds sounds of peace /
lost) on continent after continent / stanza after stanza that
ricochet / misunderstood as living as living // in my head /
i rebuild my body from the evidence / i've collected of my
existence / as fires burn like children at play / and
through the smoke / through the light breaking / through a
reluctant morning / she will say / my child came
accompanied / by dreams so vast / and i will say / i was
never taught / we mistook hope / for the horizon / bodies
breaking / for escape.

there was a stretch of a few years when i couldn't be in a room with my father without getting angry, without raising my voice and fighting with him. he'd sometimes be sitting on the couch eating peanuts and watching tv and i'd stand behind the other couch, silent until it would all come out, some random explosion triggered by nothing. it didn't matter that it hurt everyone — mom and robert and judy and, of course, my father. /// i yell less now and not just because it's a pandemic and i don't see enough people to yell at. i mean, it's gone down a lot since therapy and antidepressants. and maybe turning 50. (like you're 50. stop yelling.) i'm thinking about this today because i should be calling him and mom and asking them how the first round of their vaccination shots went but i'm just holding it off for some reason. i am afraid of their voices, the familiarity of the sounds, the length of the pauses between their words — those spaces that have trapped me and held me in joy, in pain, in this endless unknowing. /// when we lost our child my father couldn't speak to me, thought what i needed was to be left alone, for him to suffer for me in silence too, and mom kept telling me that she was praying for the child to return. such hope is long gone. but about my father — what was he ever going to teach me if i didn't become a father? what was left for him? when i was a child i thought him a giant, the thing that held the world together, like the walls in the house he built for us in seoul. /// and those years i couldn't stand to be anywhere near him, i was overwhelmed with anger above all other things, anger at him forcing me to watch him age, become less god, his body hunching and stumbling, moving toward death without telling me what i was when i was born, who i was supposed to become, what i was supposed to write, without even telling me my name.

that morning Mother was afraid / afraid of God and i held her hand / she asked me to wipe the tears from her face / as Father walked out of the room / to look for air // she does not remind me of death / the way he has all my life. / and we get to this place / where i am watching her / wondering if this is betrayal // as a child / she named me Bear / she told me / that one day / i would bash my head / into the wall / just to make it fall / like a Bear / you are Bear // we are born / and taught to erase / their names / today i wanted to / call her by it / but couldn't remember / (i could but i was / afraid that the sound / of her name escaping / my lips would make / me forget my place / in the world) // she cried / all there was / was her right hand / i didn't tell her to stop / didn't say things will be ok / faith was passed down to me / it didn't take

one day you walk out / 40 yards then a quick right like Mother tells you / then stand at the corner / to let the ones moving faster than you / cross your path / wave if there is familiarity / until it is time for you // that morning Father was upset / because the coffee was too strong / and it was you who volunteered / saying you were now old enough / to fix his dissatisfaction / and you tore away from your mother's hand / that lingered on your back a beat longer / than the days before / not even taking time to peek up at her face there will be lunch with mom and dad today / they will tell me about the denture cleaners that arrived / i will tell dad i ordered him a new pair of shoes / and he will be proud i got it at discount // there will be stories told today over soup / and roast beef and i'll ask them if they have been scheduled / for the vaccine yet // we will laugh and retell stories to break each other's hearts / and i'll thank them for teaching me to always laugh / during meals together even when the world is burning // over lunch today they will ask me about the coup / as i try to find enough strength to reach out for mom's hand / to hold her until she can stop falling / remind her of her promise to me, when i sat at the doorway / of the kitchen in korea crying, demanding that she / live til two hundred fifty // there will be lunch today with them / and i don't know what is supposed to happen / between spoonfuls of rice / when it's impossible to see the next time we gather / and laugh

i am afraid / of touch / of heat breaking / my surface / of
skin that wants / tomorrow to bloom / i am afraid / of
walking / of my body / leaving a mark / on the world / of
becoming evidence / of a crime / i am / afraid of learning /
that this is to live / of losing track / of myself again / i / am
/ afraid of her voice / telling me to learn / to remember /
the names / of the details / of a life / that exploded into /
so many details / from the start / how will it be / possible
to disappear / into the snow covered / horizon / if i can't
let go / of Mother / of Father / of Robert / of Wife / of
Daughter / of Home / i am / i am afraid / of recognizing /
her voice calling / my name

i didn't turn / didn't look back / when i walked out / of their
apartment // he stood in front of / their open door / i knew
this / waving goodbye / this i knew too // outside on
central ave / there was a korean woman / praying with
her pastor / in the driveway / in the sun // when we left
korea / when we left paraguay / when we kept leaving /
they told me about education / and opportunities / and
freedom // but they didn't show me / about touch in a land
/ that's not mine / in rooms that mispronounce / my name
until / i too forgot it / completely // before walking out of
their place / i hugged my father / that has become so
small / and sharp / his arms still awkward / around my
body // and told mom / i will see her / i will see them both
/ when the cold is gone / when we can / thaw our skin /
together // what am i to be called / when i am afraid / of
everything // what is my name / when i want to disappear
/ before i'm disappeared // will you be here / still / again /
when the summer arrives / and shuffle your feet / on the
pavement / until i recognize / the sound of being / called
home

they only saw the wolf / after they'd cut down the trees /
then hid their pale women and children / and named the
beast danger // this is the landscape upon which / father
chose to plant us — / a land too dry to to muddy / our
yellow feet with joy abandoned // they taught us killing is
no longer a sin / genocide is an inevitable tomorrow /
because erasure is an easier word / than murder, light
enough to place at / the end of a pencil as they taught /
children the first step is merely / to identify the mistake // i
don't want to tell them / not to hate me because they
should / because if i had the chance / i would strike my
bones together / and start a bonfire of their bodies /
watch new trees rise up from their ashes / while waiting
for the beasts to return // i am not angry / i am not afraid /
i am not mourning // i am nothing / i am invisible / i am
silent / as i weave through the night / into the forest
regrown // thirsty // hungry

machetes in our small hands / we walked barefoot to the sugar canes. / i don't know how many of us there were — / i only remember gabriel, his skin dark the way / i wanted my body to be, in the 110 degree sun // we broke off big pieces off and sucked the sweet / then battled the dinosaurs in the creek / as my mom cried thinking my life / would be ruined if my skin didn't stay pale / and father waited to bring the switch to my calves // those summers in paraguay, i wanted to learn to fly / but my body was on fire (mom crying to save my future) / i prayed for wings but instead my daughter was taken / to outer space quietly to float / among the celestials, trying to remember the ashes and bones / she left behind.

at school from 1st grade through grad school / through four different languages the teachers / didn't tell me about the weight of time / embedded in your body like hauntings / in this house made of bones and skin // a year lost walking on my complexion / and first footsteps at venice beach / as demarcation of assuming this life / that was meant for someone else // all the years at my father's church / filled with addicts and the lonely / i never wanted to meet god / i wanted a life extended / a life brought back / the one i was supposed to have // last night i hallucinated my daughter / asking us what she was supposed to be / what she could have been // i shuffled my feet on the rug / and soon even that small sound was gone

trying to make this morning sacred / by summoning the
ghost from the house / built by father / the dead / like me
/ will cross borders / to pretend this life continues // the
cuts on my hip and my shoulder / and thigh have
scabbed / like the branches — / stripped and hungry
outside my window // three years ago / i wanted to
identify the birds / but their colors only remind me / of the
lines on the floor of the hallways / inside the la county
hospital // what we cherish / what we long for / all end in
names we are too scared / to pronounce / what we held /
and lost / rebuilt with syllables / often clumsy and wrong //
i burned a book once / to see if she would call me / from
the fire // because i thought / to risk everything / was the
only chance / i had to see her return // i was wrong /
about this too / and the ashes too / blew away

it creeps up on me / masked as a chill / in my bones — /
this passing of a year / and i am still in the forest / even
as i can't crawl out of bed / this morning / i am still in the
forest / because this is where / i chose to lose myself /
searching for death / or my name // in the endless dark / i
reached empty hands / toward the ceiling / wanting to
clutch / one true thing / like my mother's hand / when she
told me that / it is me / she always prays for / but there
was nothing left / in the air i breathe / except my original
sin / and all the ones that came after / — god judges me /
what i hoard in my lungs / one thing has been a year now
/ and the other tragedies — / longer than that

my body waited for the sun / to break into a handful of forgettable / chapters and states away / she too is seeking peace / from the war that continues between her bones // i am listening to taylor sing / soon you'll get better / and for the first time / i don't believe her // i think my father has been lonely / in this life he chose for us all / i think this is why he told me / i needed to train myself to not need friends // i was only 10 or so / and this is maybe when the winter came / the tears too / and this body / this disappointing body // have i told you about the times i thought / i'd found a life missed inside / a phillip glass composition i was listening to / on an L train? it was snowy above i think / and when i got off at my stop in bushwick / my steps matched the violins perfectly / until i was no longer touching the world // it was long ago / it was all long ago // it is strange to miss someone / that you've never had a chance to touch / but that's what happens when the pain comes / i long for her / daughter / gone // it is so bright today / but it's still cold / and i don't believe / either of them.

every morning i make plans to call mom / my father
usually answers / he yells at her if she tries to answer /
because he is scared she will fall reaching for the phone /
he is trying in the only ways he knows — / yelling and
keeping secrets — / to keep her safe / while hiding from
all of us / the story of his heart that is tiring // the snow is
melting away / exposing patchy lawns and cats /
scampering across the street / the apartment will be
cleaned today / and maybe i will go outside, take a walk /
to pick up the burger i've been craving / judy is getting
her hair cut / and we'll talk about doctors again / oh i can't
forget to thaw the fish / before dinner time // these
morning plans / become my constant failures / because
love is unbearable / and family is the name of / what we
seldom survive / and mom / and father / and robert / and
wife and bella / and daughter / and daughter / what we
call / the shapes / of the losses / that were to come

just around the corner / mother braves the winter and the
virus / trying to fulfill the promise she made me / in the
kitchen in father's house (a house built by father) / when i
told her she must live until 250 // there is so much we
lose / so much bruising we collect / to keep from
disappointing / the ones we love the ones / whose bones
we construct / our dreams with, upon // this morning i am
looking back / i know i'm not supposed to but / there is
snow and a sheet of ice covering / everything outside and
i want to / remember my sins / the 3am escapes that end
/ with abortions and coyotes / waiting at your door /
drunken sunday mornings at church / singing to god /
asking for a quick and merciful future // she says — there
are no moles on your face / she says — your face is so
clean / i say —i don't carry all of my sins / on the surface
of skin // around the corner / just around where the

pavement breaks / into indecisions / they are loving me /
they are rooting for me / they are / all of them / losing
fragments / upon fragments / upon —

breathing / is impossible / sometimes / even or more so / when the sun / is bright through / the window // and i search / through my books / stacked clumsily / all around / the apartment // flipping through / pages / for the paragraph / that will redeem / me // but what i find / isn't salvation / but how lives / all over / have been endured / and lost // the comfort / god left us / is death / and our collective / guilt — / He even / blamed us / for his son / running away // but who do / i blame / for never getting / the chance / to hold my child // this / like all others / began with an attempt / to write about mom // this / like the other times / ends with longing / like her hand / that touches my arm / before she asks me / how i am / if i still pray / why it's so / unbearable / knowing / eternity / only comes / when we lose / all that we / have wanted / to hold / for a long / long time as a boy / then a young man / until not anything that is meant to last / i wanted to tell my mother / what i wished for / was to be someone / i could love // but i lost the only language / i could have used / to turn on the light / in our apartments bright enough / long enough / for us to how our fingers were tangled / together / to float another day in the river // i learned how to say — / thank you / to say — / may i / to say — / i am not from here / to say — / nothing as they killed me // i sleep with my arms folded / wrist bent / all clutched to my chest / and wake up confused about the pain / except that i must deserve it / then spend time typing / as if my words are trapped in my arms / and in time / my head tremors will stop / and in time / i will learn to say — / i have lost my child / to say — / my parents too are leaving / to say — / i want to be / something / that i could love / that i could love / back

in the shower / i scraped dirt off my skin / with an old razor / and wondered if death / is different under hot water // but only small cuts / opened up on / my shoulder / my hip / my thighs / and the blood came / and then dried eventually / as day turned / into gone / into leaving / into promises brought / in the dark // i feel it stinging / even in places / unharmed / i keep reaching / for my eye / checking to see if my lid / is bleeding // i woke up / missing people / i woke up / loving them / but what can such / sentiment mean / in a snow covered forest // i hear / her voice / calling me / wolf / the outline / of my body / made by / her lips // little sparks / of pain / explode on the surface / of me / and there is / so much more / left / to carry at some point it doesn't matter / if you've lived and lost here for 40 years / if you stopped here one memorable night / and ate frozen custard under a perfect sky / you are not wanted when / your skin holds the soot of the fires / they placed on your skin / your ribcage the cave that holds the hieroglyphs / stories carved with axes and tiny bones / today you rose up and felt the violence / you've contained in your bodyv— / how do you call it home / until for once / the blood soaking the soil / is not your own daughter, it's been months since i spoke to you / these days are covered in snow, places melted / hiding the cold pools of water in skies reflected / i woke up with my arms curled tight / clutching something i can no longer remember // yesterday we laughed on our walk / at the tiny footprints left on the steps of / a house around the corner / we wondered who lives there / what small lives // daughter, how does time work where you have gone / i want to say that i picture you in light / in a place more picturesque than this / but i only see your face surrounded by endless black air / how old are you now, daughter / because it's getting harder to remember / harder to forget // are you a child / are you older than me / or are you still unborn / as you were when you left // it's winter now / isn't it always so? / and we are all dying // will you return then / and claim the life / you were meant to own // walk through this world / touch the resentful texture / of a leaf still green / and cry just to feel / warmth on your face // daughter, each day i am afraid / of learning to let you go

your shoulders were always the altar / where i learned to pray and to cry / to leave offerings of more than mistakes // we were so golden for a time / our skin enough to scare us into desiring // even after the sun left for the day / i learned to trace back the shape of a shrug / through dance floors and canceled flights // your shoulder has held my face / through death and storms / until you could feed me the oxygen / that you made with your hands // even the hawk in the park / that i haven't named / in fear of watching it turn to dust / came to us to worship / this life we call ours / impossible and fragrant // to praise / to eulogize / this thing we have done / if not well / at least

with longing // your shoulders / the skin that / i was once /
so afraid to touch / i now see, my beloved / has captured
/ all of the light

i saved myself but at what cost / the holy spirit in me tells me it's time for punishment / as i choose this instead — poetry / from the safe side of a window / over and over // winter / february / is my father's voice urging me / to remain silent / to hide my intentions / to sit alone until / they all fear me // but father, i am now 50 / and so afraid of / everything that sings // last night / this morning / loved ones remind me / that we are so far from each other / fading in whispers / moving toward an end / to embrace a thing of skin // like my arms that tire / each time i write about mother / in the kitchen // i saved myself / that's what the doctor tells me / when i step away from the window // but the forest calls me again / the hawks / and branches left / stripped // the forest calls me / [father, is this fear, is this manhood] / while i celebrate time / that takes everything / everything / under the sun.

we are losing the details that make us / each day we are apart, trying to keep each other safe / from ourselves, this year of weaponized bodies. // i am forgetting my brother's voice, the shape / of his chin. when i was born he saw / all the babies at the hospital and asked my parents / if they could take every single one home because / he didn't know which one belonged to him. then he lost / his sight for days when my mother held me in her arms. // i only remember these things that were told to me. it is easier / to hold on to stories when i so long ago learned / to distrust my memories. they become lies / the minute language changed around me. / everyday there is another death or the looming of one. / i wrote of this before. i've written all of this before. / there is nothing new. but this morning it's me / sitting with my parents on their bed in our first LA apartment, / my brain still scrambling from spanish to korean to english. / you are only 10 now, they say, but life will get lonelier. / learn to be without friends, they say, learn to not need them. / we will be gone too, they say, one day when you are not 10 anymore. // we are here now. i am here now. / a time when i am no longer 10. waiting for the last / details to walk down the long hallway, faces covered, / disappear into a room, and leave me leaning / against this wall alone, writing book / after book until a final book about / the same dinner table where mother, father, brother / and i existed, // korean to spanish to english to silence.

the ground is still patchy with snow / and ice where it melted and froze overnight / but i hear her breathing, sighing / that summer has now been gone for years / is cruel in my bones — / what do we do with the time of our lives / that held death and love so closely together / that you couldn't tell them apart // last night i finally called mom to ask her about her vaccine / and she was excited telling me how her arm / was sore for a day but is ok now / and told me the date of the next round / then counted out exactly how many away that is /// that summer i turned 48 or maybe 47 / and i ran out of my meds / and spun out and down / and all the alcohol wouldn't save me // and i woke up the next morning / with a note on a bed that didn't belong to me / it said i was loved / it said things will be ok / my therapist too was trying / to keep me alive / telling me i couldn't save the world // i want to tell you today / what came after that / but i don't know what happened next — / the sun came out / or disappeared // it was warm / or it was freezing in LA // i was walking through airports / leaving or returning // i was home / i was gone / i was home // i never returned / i never left.

the therapist tells me that i have been frozen in the front yard of our house in korea but i am no longer 5 and i have to let go of the burden of saving the world and i ask her if that is the first time i wanted to die and she tells me i can't save the world, i can't save anyone but myself. /// your mouth made the shape of your mother's life — hunched over a big pot of soup and humming — and tried to sing her into joy but the words played a joke and wrapped me in fabric that made me invisible and mute until i became somebody else, exiled into a language that could never say what i meant. /// i am 7. we have been in paraguay for 2 years now. our house has a brick wall out front. i am sitting on it in the sun. this summer will be 110 degrees everyday. the man with the carriage goes by slowly, calling out to us with "sandía." i am sitting on the wall and my father is in the workroom making buttons. mom is in the house cleaning. her hair was long then. i don't know where my brother is. i am looking out on to the unpaved street. my skin is burning. i am burning. i am burning.

remembering is / screaming is / writing is / living is / losing is / feeling is / knowing is / existing is / ending is / claiming is / holding is / wanting is / longing is / hurting is / breaking is / the line is / the truth is / my skin is / your touch is / what saves me is / this snow is / what kills me is / this empty house is / your absence is / graceless is / your leaving is / what haunts me is / moving is / forgetting is / impossible is / your hand is / salvation is / your voice is / the storm is / unbearable is / this space is / empty is / my heart is / your shadow is / the night is / a scar is / your name is / this poem is / the outline of / your childhood / my fatherhood / mom's prayers / this day / letting go of / its light rue says she doesn't / think she is meant to last / in this life and is trying / so hard not to crumble // she is trying so hard to / hide her face from letting / her secrets escape // i wonder what my own face / says to everyone because / i want to tell you // that i need to hold on / to your body / even if we forget each other's names

sky / change my shape / teach me / what my father couldn't — / how to build a house / from bodies broken / by the hopes of others // salt air / tangle my hair / unwieldy / in the wind / unexpected / like 50 years / of a life / i never planned for // melody / bend this passing time / we are / losing so much / more than / we can grasp // breaths / stay in our hands / held / with forgiveness // breaths / gasp / as our hearts / learn to say / farewell my father looks at my new nikes when i come over and wonders if he should buy a nice pair of shoes for once even though he no longer goes on a nightly walk with mom. it's odd thinking of someone's final pair of shoes. what color would my father's be? // in days i will be gone. we will promise each other to hug soon, hold inside the goodbyes we aren't ready for because sometimes prayers never leave our bodies, never pass through the atmosphere — how can they save a child born a wolf, their youngest only because the next ones were lost. // we built this family on silence but there was a brief period when my parents told me stories, their stories, of the wars and the marriage that came after. // now we are returning to keeping secrets from each other about bones and hearts breaking, of pills that keep us alive. they don't know how to talk to me about regrets. i don't know how to tell them about longing.

the days between / the breaking / and the poem // searching for words / that were already / tucked in / your body // these ribs / a cage / that holds / a heart / this beating bird / in mourning // the two things / that ever belonged / to me — / my name / and the other / we call the ending // one long lost / the other not / yet here // all the windows / that called / for me / in different cities — / seoul / asunción / los angeles / san clemente / new york / pittsburgh // the pavement / that opens up / its cracked black / bosom // it would have been / so easy / it was always so impossible // it was never / my intent to leave / on this journey / nor yours // but your feet move / to survive / until the road / becomes hidden / under the snow / this path / like white death // their voices — / mom

/

father / your lost child / disappearing into / the silence /
that consumes everything / in this never-ending / winter //
a wolf / alone / running then walking / into the forest // to
rest.

we were found / under my desk in an apartment / too big for the two of us / in downtown los angeles // and we said / we didn't care that she was gone / that we didn't want kids anyway / that we were choosing us // there was freedom / for all the things to come / until i wanted to die / until the panic attacks returned // we forgot for a short time / that we are held by / the things we lose born in days frozen until the remnants of wars became hidden under our feet // the sun reshaped my shadow and taught me a life of disappointments // there is a man yelling at his child because he wants to run off across the street ahead of his family // was there a message / were there words moving through the bare branches / do you ever think about me? / do you return for me // do you consider my body / do you consider my heart // am i just a slight thing you rustled on your journey back to god?

standing at the window / my naked body brightened by the snow /// a friend tells me of an apartment available on st marks / for only $1500. /// i dream too / of better places / of joy / of a past that isn't distorted / by pain /// have i ever damaged someone / i didn't claim to love / have i ever screamed at someone / that didn't love me /// last night i dreamt of an onion / it was put in my hand and it was dirty / i put it under the running tap and washed / layers and layers of it / i don't know who it belonged to / who it was that handed it to me / i don't know why i washed it /// it snowed all night like it snowed / the night before but it melts fast / because it's not cold enough / i am told it's been raining in LA / and mom and dad are supposed to get their shots today /// mom told me on the phone the other day that / dad received the shoes i got him / and he is walking around the apartment / a smile stuck on his face / talking about how he got new shoes / from his son / i hope he wears it today / when he goes to get his shot /// this winter will end one day / and then everything else will arrive /// my mother unable to walk / naps and smiles / prays for her sons /// my mother / she deserved a much better life.

hope / was always / the hammer / i wielded / against / my body / because i wanted / a say / in my unmooring. // my father / was a builder / who raised walls / around us only / to trap / the ghosts inside / until it all began / to come / apart / with his first fall / from a ladder. // i am blurry eyed / pulling bones / off the hinges / waiting to hear / a doctor in pasadena / that i will not be / able to have / a child / sketching the shape / of another life / while lying under my desk. // hope / was always / the sound of / the lies / we told / each other / that this was / freedom / this will let us / do whatever / we want // what have / we done? / where did freedom / take us / except to / pittsburgh and a pandemic // and this hammer / i swing / at everything / at every one close / enough for me / to touch // the lines that broke / in mom's eye / the heart that pauses / in dad's chest // hope / is this snow / that i walk into mute / convinced that / a voice / god or some unturned / rock polished / years of stillness / is waiting / to save me // i am tired / and so are you / of believing / in the sun / that lies / to your skin // tell me, nightfall / is there a secret / in this dark silent / moment // tell me, nightfall / what did i / lose from my life / today / while hidden in / the light like these hands / of mine / trembling without / thought / the lakes / oscillate / from empty / to holding the weight / of all the promises / god / portended // we are reaching / into the dark / part of january / to capture / something / akin to salvation / to food / to bodies forming / and reforming / into unbreakable / forms // once / we anticipated / birth / and mobiles / spinning light / unto the surface / of our world / names called / in the middle / of tired nights / tethering us / to a future // the fall / the winter // the loss / isn't a loss / like the lakes / that held / our bodies / until they couldn't // what is true / on wednesday / is gone by thursday / and something about / the unwashed sheets / will hold me / in my own scent / and the shape of / all that is gone // sing / sing / sing // the shape of / all / that is gone when you are a child / your parents don't ask you / how you feel about leaving / the only home you've known // they tell you that / this is for you / your future / and your eventual past / calling it legacy / as if it was yours // you are in the front yard / and it is winter / snowing / because the cold stays / in your memory / like the ghost inside the house / waiting for you / to grow into a man / and learn who she is // it is winter / and they will find you / hiding / with the dog in her house / and they will tell you a story / that you will believe you remember / only to one day / become a lie / a story that becomes a fish / only to become a tree // this is vague / but not the important part / it is the day before christmas / and tomorrow i will sit / in their tiny rent control apartment / and the three of us / no brother / no wife / no dogs / the three of us around plates of / fried chicken / not seasoned enough / because your mother is / slowly losing her ability to taste / to tolerate salt // mother's face will tell you / the stories of the babies / that she expected to be crying / on the floor / their faces like yours / and father's hunched posture / will tell you how he blames / himself for your broken body / and this silence / this silence // will touch your skin / and you'll ask it / how to help them / disappear without their disappointments / or your legacy / how to hold them up / to the light and take them back / home.

i was frozen / long before the winter / came and the leaves / had gone. // at 5 i didn't know / how to ask god / or father why // it is impossible / to stay intact when / your body is made / to cross borders / before you learn / of nations and the limits / of your skin // at 14 i never wanted / to make it to 15 / or a winter watching / my parents struggling to make / it across the room // at 50 i call for the ghost / of the woman who / haunted me in that house / (again) / built by father // call for everyone i didn't / know i would lose / at 50 i walk out into / a patch of sun / with a sleepy cat / and thaw my body / frozen still // so many borders away you will learn that the ghost in the house father built was always the daughter you would one day lose and the footprints you left behind were covered up and gone // you were a wolf without a language trying to move your body forward until this loneliness of life sounded like your mother laughing again, singing — my stupid boy — laughing and singing to me — my stupid silly boy.

i ask him what his plans are with his heart that keeps slowing down while he washes his face in the bathroom. // the doctor tells him it is too risky now for the surgery that is needed, to open his chest up again, with his age and the virus. // he gets up from the couch and asks me to help him change the ringtone on his new phone, asks why netflix is asking for more money, asks me to take him to the fifth floor laundry room and teach him how to put money on the card for the new washer and dryer. // he is walking back and forth. i get up and slide open the back door and step out on the balcony. their succulents have grown so much, but there isn't enough sun for flowers, mom says and tucks a 20 dollar bill in my hand for xmas. // i nod and return to the dining table pushed into the corner by the front door. their next door neighbor died. he fell backward and broke his skull. he was 92. and someone smashed the main entrance. // i put my shoes on and my hoodie and say goodbye, i will see you on new year's, and mom shrugs because my brother won't be coming. "i tell myself that i won't die," dad says, "i tell myself i can't die because i need to take care of your mom. that's my plan." // i wave back and walk out, turn back from the hallway, as he stands outside their door and waves at me, mom somewhere still inside, sitting on a chair, her left hand on the table, her feet dangling off the floor she can't quite reach. // i wave back then turn, adjust my mask, put my hands in my pockets, and walk out into an empty los angeles street.

whenever my father came home after a night out drinking / he brought home french pastries and slept alone in the other room / he didn't want us to smell the alcohol sweating out from his skin / i didn't really know him when he was still drinking — / he quit in paraguay, where we used the johnny walker bottles / he'd emptied as water bottles / all i knew was that i was happy about the pastries // he'd tell us what a treat they were, how expensive / they were at the time in korea / and how we should never start drinking // there was a night at a party after a soccer match / where these grown men came up to me drunk / yelling at me, cursing my father, asking me / if my father thought he was too good for them or something / because he wasn't drinking with them anymore / i just shrugged, smiled, and told myself that i would / find them when i was no longer 7 years old / and burn their homes down into ash // my brother texted me to tell me he got his first shot, the dolly parton one / and i remember how mad my parents are with him / because they haven't seen him in over a year even though / he lives a mile away, mad at him / and also sad for him because he's always been a germaphobe // family is such strange architecture / family by biology, by proximity, by migration / how we learn to support each other even though / we are not connected by blood / how we learn to plunder each other after a smile // my father hit me with a baseball bat when i was in high school / he caught me stoned out of my mind in my room / and i feared him more than i loved him for most of my life / fear has been replaced with anger, not because he hit me / but because his body is failing and he seems so close to the end // violence, like family, is wrapped around my bones / like a tourniquet, like an old segment of rusted chain that / a tree has grown its skin over // like that day the man from an opposing soccer team / showed up at our house in paraguay with a gun / me sitting on the floor next to mom who was on the rocking chair / the man with the gun demanding to see my father // i sat there playing with buttons / as mom told the man my father wasn't home and / he should sit and wait for him if he really needed to shoot him // after a few minutes the man left, uncomfortable and embarrassed // it's morning and i'm drinking morning wine / which is wine you drink before noon / and robert texted me and a kid / across the street is playing on the swing // i'm waiting for the bakery to call me to tell me / the baguettes are ready and the sun always / reminds me of violence / and violence, like love, reminds me of family / of immigration / of all the inevitable things in this life.

the noise in my head exhausts me and keeps me up at night. i scream into the pillow until it is 2018 again and at the therapist's office for the first time, my face in my hands trying to catch and shove my tears back inside me, screaming "i want to die, i want to die, all i want is to die." i scream it, then, now, this morning, this dark, looking for the path that takes me to contentment. // i don't know why my heart longs for this time when i was the most alone. i walk because the noises in my head tonight won't let me breathe. i need the snow to bury me, quick steps until there is nothing left but the white silence. i believed this is where i'd find my nameless child. i walk to catch her shifting on a stoop that she calls home as her life unfolds in the streets ahead of her, i walk into the winter that whistles something that could be her name. // today i want it to be dorothea because that's what my favorite singer sings and it is a beautiful name, a perfect name, something that i imagine would feel comfortable leaving my heart each day. i walk. i walk into it, this dying that comes too soon and too slow. the noise in my head this morning is blinding me. i want to — i want to — all i want is to — // dorothea. dorothea. if i say this name enough, will you come back to us? dorothea. dorothea. if we sing your name, will you stay and share your life with us even if it's for the briefest of time, for one perfect day?

then the words came after the languages / and they were bricks / they were bullets / they were bones of bodies i didn't recognize // i can't remember right now if i ever / learned the spanish words for pain or betrayal / while barefoot on the burning streets outside our house in / asunción, the ones that would flood with each / storm. by morning of my 40th year in // this country of a sun that lies / about the dark nights to come the birds didn't / even show up, nor the neighbor who sings badly / passing our bedroom window on her walk because / the workers are here to tear out the curb in all four / corners of our intersection while finding / a way to continue their lives. i want // to return to the words that i tried to wield / as shards of metal of glass strong / enough to carve into fresh cement / the name i hear whispered to me from the woods / of mother of lover of daughter of the ghost who / has followed me across borders. is this // another language, the one that knows how to spell my name / in the storm? and when she calls me wolf / the snow falling to mute my death // wraps me in a peace that my heart my legs never afforded me.

my father gave me a bible / and a set of highlighters / and
told me to read / mark it with a different color / each time
a verse stood out to me / the book is still on my shelf /
many years and cities and homes / later — / the thin
nearly translucent pages / punctuated by / bright yellow
green pink / lines made by my hands // over the years / i
read it from cover to cover / four times / sometimes
finding a glimpse of god / most often not // i will tell you /
the book of jeremiah / was always the most difficult to get
through / but i don't know why // the most painful years /
were the ones when / my father held service for his
church / in the tiny living room of our apartment / in
koreatown — / our home invaded each week / by terrible
people / who wanted to be saved / or just wanted my
parents to pray for them / before they headed out to
vegas again / to test god's willingness / to bless them //
one night my face flush / and wet with crying / i told my
parents / we needed to abandon them / abandon them all
/ because we weren't meant / to carry the weight / of
other people's longing // the magnolias bloomed and
wilted / so fast this year across the street / the flowers
unable to withstand / the erratic pittsburgh weather / it is
very still outside / it makes me feel like i'm waiting / for
something beyond my comprehension // call it mercy / or
whatever it was that leapt / from those pages / my father
gave me / each time i flipped through them / leaving my
own etchings / a trail of bread crumbs / for me to follow /
find breaths that resemble / all that is holy / or for god / to
return to me / and apologize / for once / for what they
have wrought —

undone /// undoing /// between bones between breaths lost to panic /// skin // sin /// what makes me is inescapable /// where is my forest / that annihilates / then soothes my body / with ice / with an endless winter /// undone /// untouched /// how will i recognize the life i have lived / scattered on pavement / cracking under the weight of all / that has been killed /// the flowers / in their second bloom // the beginning of another loss /// undone /// unmade /// unforgiven /// we were happy / a time a place / that exists less each day / there are photos that tell me / this story can be true /// undone // soon // undone /// you say my name / place a lifeboat / between the letters / that have spelled me / wrong /// undone /// shattered across life / and lifetimes /// i don't know where this goes /// i can't remember how i began /// undone /// how do i begin to love myself / this thing so long /// undone

i want it all to end even if it means death / it isn't pain but the fear of it returning to ravage my body / i keep falling asleep on the couch, work that's due on my lap / the ceiling fan slow above me to control the fire // i think of my mother who likes to say my name / in the middle of sentences as she is talking to me / as if to remind me to stay a little longer / sometimes she seems so small that i want to lift her in my pretty hands / so the aliens can take her away / just as she has always dreamed of // i am drifting away / slowly as it is / until not even my mother will be able / to bring me back / not even my name nested / on her tongue // the world / means to take away / everything / until there is nothing / left / of survival // but this desire / to choose how / how my poem / ends when i was a child, 2 or 3, in seoul, i stood / at the foot of the steps that led to the second floor / in the house my father built for his family / and cried. i've told this story so many times, to friends / and lovers, to readers through poems / and stories. i cried because i saw a woman sitting on / the steps staring at me, her mouth moving, speaking / in ways i couldn't hear. i am 50 now and i am starting / to hear her, the words she was saying to me back / then. she was telling me that i would give birth to her, that i would / write her into being, because i am a writer and writers / make ghosts. and now i am trying to listen again, to hear / the rest of what she said, why i needed her to visit / the child me, what it is that i needed her to tell me. / there is a breeze and the windows are open. i walked / outside and bought a bread. this morning my skin feels / the world dissolving and it feels / like heartbeats. it feels invisible. my body — this / morning — feels alive like it all does near the end.

when you left — / when they took you / the only thing i wanted was the loss to embrace me // how do i tell my heart that broke / you simply exited / the outline of my life / that you are thriving / in worlds that i've only dreamt of / in space / where my mother / has always dreamt of visiting /// years later / when you came to me / standing in the light beside / my bed — waving / (all grown you were: beautiful beyond) / i saw your lips move / utterances that have haunted me / you, her // it took me so long / to see that it was you / all along / in seoul / on our steps / having come back to my childhood / to tell me something / that could undo me // writing / has been my ongoing attempt / to hear you / each stanza / another chance / at meeting your voice abducted / displaced / then / misplaced / your body an object / lost / it learns to breathe / differently / because you can't / let them know you / are still alive // you learn histories / that were never true / nor did it belong / to you / you learn to / shape your tongue / into lies / until even you / begin to / believe // but pretty sounds / from your lips / after you tamed your howls / never were enough / for them to / love you / and the coldness / of the window / in an unexpected april / reminds you / how you will fight / now / to never belong / to them // you are born / with two things / all yours — / your body / of connected / imperfections / and your death / to come // they convinced you / one is broken / and you have failed / by loving it // the other / your greatest fear / to run from / everyday / for the rest of / your mortgaged life // snow / touches / bewildered bodies / today / the wind / sideways / like a question / forbidden: // what is it / that your dying / has held / so valuable / that they have / worked so hard / to steal / from your heart the fires came. then the rain. and today the breeze. but it all lingers together. everyone is trying to wear the joy that once belong to the ones they killed and call it homage or memorial or a book. past midnight i am trying to teach my legs to cut the air that holds me. the rain — i tell my mother of it as she tells me about her fall from bed. there was good news and bad like this light that is neither brilliant or sacred.

she pushes a plate of daikon inches closer to me, her eyes fixed on my every movement, making sure she doesn't miss a single instance of me eating her food, when my father is on the couch watching pirated korean drama on youtube, that i wonder if she is shrinking. // it's sunday of christmas week of the hardest year we've had as a family. they haven't seen my brother, their eldest son, who is trapped in his apartment, sick, afraid, in 9 months even though he lives a mile away. and i've been gone in the midwest. the bones in my wife's body has been unraveling all year. // i stare at mom's left eye, blackened from another fall. she will never find her balance again so dad yells at her because he's afraid of what's to come. // when i finish the soup, she asks if i want an orange. i say yes. some coffee? a piece of cake? i say yes to everything. to everything. another meal. yes. // she says she misses bella and how the three legged dog hopped around their apartment until she could no longer. // there was another fall on the sidewalk and a masked woman asking if she could help my father pick her up. // and i smile, eat another wedge as she uses the camera of the new phone i got her to check on her black eye, telling me it's not as bad as it was 2 days ago when she tried to get up from the couch and fell face first, her glasses pushing against her. // i don't know why she always falls face first, dad says, demonstrating how it happened. // i keep smiling, laughing even. sip of bad coffee and a slice of a spongy cake from one of the hundreds of korean bakeries around LA. i smile because for the longest time my family, even my brother robert, believed that i had the power to wish things to life — even save the life of a grandfather who was ashamed of me. // i point at an appointment written on their calendar. // your father had to see the doctor about his heart, mom says. // he's struggling to breathe, she says. // i collapsed in the bathroom the other day because i couldn't breathe, he says. // and in the kitchen too, she says. // doctor says it's too risky right now for surgery, she says. // you should try this new ramen we bought, he says. // ok, dad, i say. // one day i'll go to sleep and won't wake up and that's how it will end, he says // all my life i've been trying to figure out who i am, through languages and geography, but what does it matter when the winter comes in the loneliest year and you shatter.

becoming a writer / to become a maker of ghosts / as if /
trauma would not find me if i ran // over 30 years of
writing / and here i am / just about where i began / still
unable to know / what my parents carry on their backs
bent // on facebook i saw the news from many months
ago / that the korean war was officially over // what little
has changed / changes / when we are born to destroy
each other // judy says / that she's been seeing the ghost
/ more often lately in the hallway / of our apartment / and
this morning i mistook the wind / for something i can't
reach // i keep washing the dishes / soil them again / and
miracles / like fatherhood / are just things / that i was
taught / to want // the words i type are / getting quieter /
when everyone i reach for / is crying // i want to want /
once more — // for the skyline / of the city that was
promised us / to rise on the skin of your shoulder /
burning quietly in the sun / like the untamed desert / as
you lie / on your side by the window / waiting to hear /
your name / that left my lips so long / ago

at best / we will lose each other / at something we have been taught / to call the end. // but look / not beyond the rubble / the destruction that became / of our lives / but in it, in the heart of it // the skeleton that rises / into silence / bones of houses and arms / that were our walls / ladders through all of it // don't believe them / when they tell you / there is nothing above us / but god // go / climb up / and find the room / and you will see what is left of our city / our home / the life we had / through the one wall that has / been destroyed // look around / do you see the bricks on the floor / rebuild it and call this place immaculate // there will be no god / nor angels / nor anything invisible they asked us / to believe in // instead / on the balcony / you will see a body / walking toward you / and a face that peeks in / with a smile // and you will say / i know your name / i have known your name // and one by one / we will arrive / and gather / and rebuild all of it / with our names // rejoice // we will rejoice // sing the songs / of our names / and fill the skies / with laughter.

the air / with the season / reimagines / the shape of me /
bringing terror / familiar / like the light // when you are
ready / break my surface / with your tongue on fire /
swallow the earth / inside me / until you find my home // i
am lost / where bones / intersect / i have been lost /
endlessly / even reaching / the water / at the edge / of the
world / only to find / the brutality / of a horizon // these
hands / open / the trembles / are my language / trying to
tell you / that the land / is your skin / browned / pulsing / a
rhythm / that god / has prayed for / that this wreckage / is
my body / in an endless war / with my heart

when you were a child / they taught you about the winter / pointing at the dog hanging / frozen from your balcony. / now it is night in some year much later // and you have been standing / too long in the snow / that silences your life for once // sometimes you are a fire burning / sometimes you are just the memory of burning / and sometimes you are the form / of your mother tilting uncontrollably / to one side as she reaches for you.

i caught the smoke / in my mouth / as the world burned / the residue of statuary / dissolving on my tongue / like the questions to jesus / i couldn't release in the temples // today — the sun the fire / the scent of becoming the past / tomorrow — how winter / returns in april / as if god isn't fallible // even the sacred / loses time between its ribs / and calls it rebirth / calls it salvation / or another form / of inescapable pain // how funny it all is — / digging your own root / from the soil that you called home / to become less than the pigment / of another's skin // please — let me go / alone into the shade / of the final trees / this winter forest / of angry branches / bare and silent // don't ask me to stay / tethered to the violent hands / you wield like hope / don't ask me / to run back to / the story you meant to write / of my death // my name is / the monster / you taught the world / to fear we will pause a little longer before the next touch, my hand on your swollen knee, until this space is vast enough to cradle those things we were trying to wish into existence — our child growing up on the streets on new york, running to subway stations few yards ahead of us ready to show us how big she was getting, how she could travel through our world alone now, introducing her to every shop owner and doorman and fruit vendor so she'd feel all of this was hers even if it was never ours. we will pause another day, another week between pittsburgh mornings staring out our windows at the falling snow in a city that was never meant for us, a city that left us unmoored and broken until there was nothing left but the warm skin of your palms on my face. it is a bright cold and i stand in the sun and tell myself that i have destroyed so many things and people in this unremarkable life and called it love or art or unrelenting grief. sometimes like today and this winter that is too bright i tell myself it was for the best that she is in outer space, floating eternally, away from me and my hands that break everyone they touch. i will drink until there is no more hope of remembering her name. i will tell mother and father that this longest of years will be a little longer.

in the kitchen / i only heard music / but the music / was just the sound of the ocean / emptying out of my heart / i told my feet to dance / i told this terror / to cry / there was nothing / but this body / these feet shuffling / this body / this body swaying / and i don't know / if it was how it ends / or / the beginning of another life / in the kitchen under two broken light bulbs / i was there / trying to dance / trying to cry / and then / i was gone / then / i was gone and then / i was / gone / i was gone / and then i / was gone was gone i / then i was gone and / then i was gone / i was gone / gone / and i was gone.

Chiwan Choi is the author of 4 books of poetry,
The Flood, and the Daughter Trilogy — *Abductions*,
The Yellow House, and *my name is wolf*.
He wrote, presented, and destroyed the novel
Ghostmaker throughout the course of 2015.
He is a partner at Writ Large Projects.

Chiwan was born in Seoul, Korea,
spent his early childhood in Asunción, Paraguay,
and now splits his time between
Pittsburgh, PA and Los Angeles, CA.

Published by
Writ Large Press
a division of Writ Large Projects
writlargeprojects.com

ISBN: 978-1-945178-24-5

Cover art by
Ana Chaidez

Written & Designed by
Chiwan Choi

★

★

daughtertrilogy.com

www.ingramcontent.com/pod-product-compliance
Lightning Source LLC
Chambersburg PA
CBHW071953100426
42736CB00043B/3142